## Money Matters

# Spending and Saving

By Mary Hill

SCHOLASTIC INC.

New York  Toronto  London  Auckland  Sydney
Mexico City  New Delhi  Hong Kong  Buenos Aires

Photo Credits:  Cover © Photodisc/Getty Images; pp. 5, 21 (top left) © Paul Barton/Corbis; p. 7
© ROB & SAS/Corbis; pp. 9, 21 (top right) © Tom Bean/Corbis; p. 11 © Chip Henderson/Index Stock Imagery, Inc.; pp. 13, 21 (bottom left) © Roy Morsch/Corbis; p. 15 © Paul Barton/Corbis;
pp. 17, 21 (bottom right) © Chuck Savage/Corbis; p. 19 © SuperStock

Contributing Editor: Shira Laskin
Book Design: Mindy Liu

ISBN 0-516-24893-6

12 11 10 9 8 7 6 5 4 3 2                           5 6 7 8 9 10/0

Printed in  Mexico                                        61

# Contents

There are many kinds of jobs.

Some people work in stores.

Some people work outside.

People can **save** the money
they **earn**.

They can save money
in a **bank**.

People can save their money in **piggy banks** too.

People can also **spend** their money.

They can spend money on a house.

HOME FOR SALE
BY APPOINTMENT

15

People also spend money on food.

Sometimes people spend money on **supplies** for school.

It is fun to learn about spending and saving money.

# New Words

bank  (**bangk**) a place where people save
their money

earn  (**uhrn**) to get money for working at a job or for
working in some other way

piggy banks  (**pig**-ee **bangks**) toy banks in the shape
of a pig in which people save coins

save  (**sayv**) to keep something because you want to
have it or do something with it later

spend  (**spend**) to use

supplies  (suh-**plyze**) things needed to do something

# To Find Out More

**Books**
*All about Money*
by Natalie M. Rosinsky
Compass Point Books

*Earning Money*
by Tanya Thayer
Lerner Publishing Group

**Web Site**
**Savings Bonds for Kids**
http://www.publicdebt.treas.gov/sav/savkids.htm
Learn about saving money and play games on this Web site.

# Index

**About the Author**
Mary Hill is a children's book author. She has written books about many different subjects.

**Reading Consultants**
Kris Flynn, Coordinator, Small School District Literacy, The San Diego County Office of Education

Shelly Forys, Certified Reading Recovery Specialist, W.J. Zahnow Elementary School, Waterloo, IL

Paulette Mansell, Certified Reading Recovery Specialist, and Early Literacy Consultant, TX